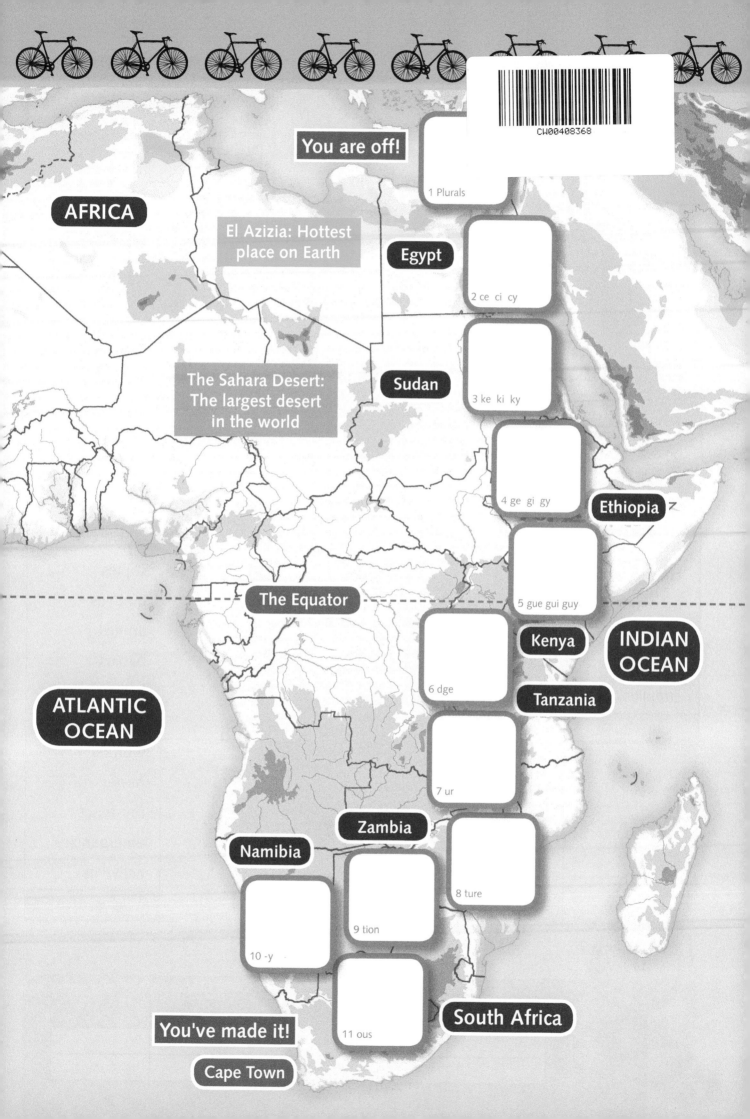

Plurals

Read the words.

Set 1 (11 words)	Add es You can hear the extra syllable. Set 2 (17 words)	Only these 7 common words ending in 'o' must have es. Set 3 (12 words)	f/fe → ves when you hear a /v/ sound. Set 4 (12 words)	y → ies unless there is a vowel before the y. Set 5 (17 words)
foxes	kisses	potatoes	knives	spies
elves	misses	tomatoes	wives	flies
boxes	losses	embargoes	shelves	tries
tomatoes	bosses	heroes	wolves	lies
potatoes	bushes	vetoes	hooves	cries
strawberries	crashes	echoes	lives	replies
cherries	ashes	torpedoes	halves	copies
loaves	brushes	**These usually end 'es' (but 's' is acceptable):**	calves	bunnies
watches	mixes		thieves	armies
volcanoes	witches	buffaloes	scarves	babies
supplies	matches	dominoes	leaves	ladies
11 words so far	ditches	mosquitoes	sheaves	fairies
	patches	tornadoes	**52 words so far**	worries
	benches	volcanoes		ferries
	lunches			mysteries
	wishes	**For other words ending in 'o', you can just add 's'. Hurrah!**		emergencies
	dishes			activities
	28 words so far	**40 words so far**		**69 words so far**

	up to 39 Sparking	40–49 Glowing	50–59 Burning	60–69 Sizzling	70+ Red hot!
Score/Date					
Score/Date					

Read the story then draw the picture.

The foxes and elves had packed their boxes full of bright red tomatoes, roast potatoes, huge strawberries, sweet cherries and loaves of fresh bread. Just as they were looking at their watches, the two volcanoes nearby erupted and all their supplies flew up into the air!

Practise writing.

Build your word power.

Brilliant! You are off!

Egypt: You set off from Cairo on a wonderfully flat road; there are pyramids in the desert and all round are fields irrigated by the Nile, the longest river in the world.
Your charities are chosen and months of training completed. All your camping equipment has to be packed onto your bike along with a camera, electronics, clothes, sunglasses, maps, diaries, phrasebooks, penknives, your passport and, of course, a first aid kit with loads of insect repellent to keep away flies and mosquitoes!

ce ci cy

Soft c

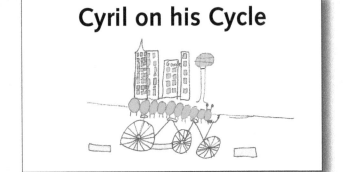

Cyril on his Cycle

By Lucas

Read the words.

Set 1 (13 words)	Set 2 (20 words)	Set 3 (20 words)	Set 4 (20 words)	Set 5 (20 words)
December	once	substance	hindrance	discipline
Cyril	place	difference	cemetery	excellent
centipede	dance	exciting	existence	recently
decided	race	decimal	sacrifice	celebrate
cycle	ice	scientist	prejudice	sincerely
city	nice	century	necessary	percentage
success	space	experience	convenience	decisive
since	cell	certain	cider	fascinate
police	chance	circle	proceed	glacier
notices	force	recent	ceiling	acceptance
icy	scene	bicycle	accept	circumstance
exercise	sentence	medicine	misplace	certainly
accident	pencil	mice	precede	cinnamon
13 words so far	decide	percent	cereal	incident
	office	service	recipe	accuracy
	practice	conceal	decision	concentration
	science	descend	successful	exceedingly
	process	cyclone	cinema	participate
	except	central	celery	circulation
	distance	cyclist	cylinder	anticipated
	33 words so far	53 words so far	73 words so far	93 words so far

One Minute Wonders

	up to 39 Sparking	40–49 Glowing	50–59 Burning	60–69 Sizzling	70+ Red hot!
Score/Date					
Score/Date					

6

Read the story then draw the picture.

It was December and Cyril the Centipede decided to cycle around the city. It was not a success since the police had put up notices everywhere saying, "Too icy!" Too late for Cyril. His exercise ended in an accident.

Practise writing.

Build your word power.

Well done!
ous
-y
tion
ture
ur
dge
gue gui guy
ge gi gy
ke ki ky
ce ci cy
Plurals

Brilliant! You made it to the next stage!

Sudan: It's extremely hot! Since you are in danger of dehydration and sunstroke, it is necessary to keep drinking lots of water. Cycling is an exceedingly good way to learn about the country as you can stop and explore and you are certain to chat with all sorts of people. Sights, smells and sounds are all around you. You also keep fit by taking lots of exercise and you can cover a good distance easily. Bicycles are simple to fix, free to run and are harmless to the environment.

ke ki ky

Kitten in the Ketchup

By Charles

Read the words.

Set 1 (11 words)	Set 2 (20 words)	Set 3 (20 words)	sk Set 4 (20 words)	sk Set 5 (20 words)
king	**kill**	kebab	**skin**	skinny
kitten	**kick**	kidney	**sky**	skittles
Kipper	**kiss**	kitted	**skirt**	skewbald
keep	**key**	kilo	**skill**	skimming
kind	keen	kidneys	skid	skinflint
Kit	kid	kennel	skim	skittered
skipped	kilt	kilted	skip	skittish
kite	kissed	kidded	skimp	skivvy
kitchen	kip	kidding	sketch	skylark
skidding	keel	kindly	skipped	skywrite
ketchup	Kent	kibbutz	sketched	skydive
11 words so far	kiln	kilos	skimmed	skyscraper
	killed	kindle	skilled	skibobber
	kettle	kennels	skewed	skeleton
	kidnap	kind-hearted	unskilled	skinniest
	kernel	kidnapper	skirmish	skeletal
	kidnapped	kerfuffle	skitter	skedaddle
	kinship	handkerchief	skittle	skinnier
	kiwi	kick-started	skimpy	skirmishes
	kick-off	kedgeree	skirting	semi-skilled
	31 words so far	51 words so far	71 words so far	91 words so far

One Minute Wonders

	up to 39 Sparking	40–49 Glowing	50–59 Burning	60–69 Sizzling	70+ Red hot!
Score/Date				6ə	
Score/Date					

Read the story then draw the picture.

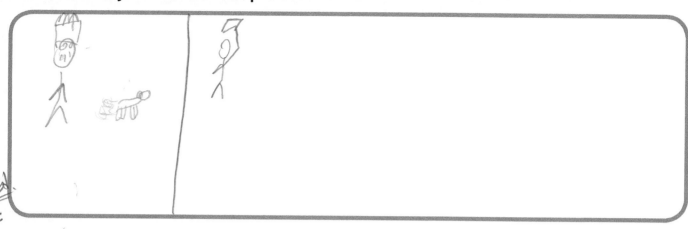

The king had lost his little kitten, Kipper.

"I wanted to keep him safe," he cried. His kind son, Kit, skipped in with a lovely kite to make him feel better. The next moment, they heard a crash in the kitchen, rushed to have a look and saw the kitten skidding in the ketchup!

Practise writing.

The kint X king had lost his little kitten, kipper.
"I wanted to keep safe," he cried. His kind som, kit, skipped
i with a lovely kite to make him happy feel better.
The next moment, they head

Build your word power.

Brilliant! You made it to the next stage!

South Sudan: You must push your bike up huge sun-kissed sand dunes! Dealing with extreme heat is tough on the body and your skin can burn easily but you learn to adapt. Water is a big issue, though. There are regular water cuts and in rural areas pumps are often broken or locked, except during certain hours, to avoid wastefulness. The people are very skilled at carrying the water on their heads. Luckily, the locals are very kind to you and you fill up your water containers whenever you can.

Soft g

Gentle Giant in the Gym

By Heather

Read the words.

Set 1 (11 words)	Set 2 (20 words)	Set 3 (20 words)	Set 4 (20 words)	Set 5 (20 words)
George	large	suggest	engage	interchange
gentle	age	privilege	genie	religion
giant	change	average	rigid	prearrange
gigantic	stage	vegetable	surgeon	geography
gym	danger	exaggerate	register	digestible
suggested	general	language	messenger	manageable
gypsy	strange	gymnast	oxygen	generously
huge	imagine	giraffe	angelic	biology
energy	wage	gesture	tragedy	energetic
magic	gem	tragic	fugitive	registering
legend	barge	pigeon	refugee	emergency
11 words so far	page	angel	urgently	original
	charge	Egypt	genius	illogical
	plunge	margin	digestion	tragically
	germ	ginger	allergy	belligerent
	bulge	submerge	regiment	gesticulate
	logic	arrange	gentleness	non-chargeable
	urgent	exchange	chargeable	imagination
	village	manage	logical	exaggeration
	engine	digest	engagement	indigestible
	31 words so far	51 words so far	71 words so far	91 words so far

	up to 39 Sparking	40–49 Glowing	50–59 Burning	60–69 Sizzling	70+ Red hot!
Score/Date					
Score/Date					

Read the story then draw the picture.

George, the gentle giant, wanted to be gigantic.
"Go to the gym," suggested the elderly gypsy.
Soon George was huge and filled with energy.
"It's magic!" he shouted. "I will be a legend!"

Practise writing.

Build your word power.

Well done!
ous
-y
tion
ture
ur
dge
gue gui guy
ge gi gy
ke ki ky
ce ci cy
Plurals

Brilliant! You made it to the next stage!

Ethiopia: You've crossed the legendary Sahara, the biggest desert in the world. It is huge! Remember your chain needs cleaning and oiling every day or it is in danger of clogging up from the dust. The vegetation changes to forest and it is a privilege to see colobus monkeys in the trees. What a magical sight! This is a very religious country and the language is called Amharic.

# Sizzling Syllables! ①

Read the syllables.

Six syllable types

Closed	ban	ren	em	pon	cup	riv	pat	mim	tod	dom
Open	ta	re	so	pre	ho	pe	bi	la	me	co
Evil e	ake	ete	ile	ome	ule	ane	epe	ise	oze	upe
Vowel	bai	way	fee	rea	goa	low	goo	few	cue	lew
-r	par	ser	for	nar	der	vor	ard	cer	tar	nor
-le	-ble	-cle	-dle	-fle	-gle	-kle	-ple	-tle	-zle	-sle

Got it? ☐

Cycle Africa patterns

cem	gest	kit	gi	cess	ket	gend
ace	cen	ger	cit	cir	age	ken
kip	gen	keb	cer	kid	cise	gion
gic	cy	kee	gyp	sci	kin	cid

Got it? ☐

Prefixes and suffixes

-ing	mis-	re-	dis-	-al	im-	-ful
-ment	inter-	de-	-est	non-	-y	-ed
pre-	ness	-ity	pro-	-ly	il-	un-
-en	sub-	-er	-less	semi-	-able	be-

Got it? ☐

Fiery Phrases! (1)

Foxes and Boxes	Cyril on his Cycle	Kitten in the Ketchup	Gentle Giant in the Gym
	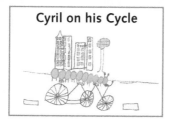		

Read the phrases.

Set 1	Set 2	Set 3
two loaves, please	what a success	a quick sketch
pass those brushes	cease fire	a bright blue skirt
listen to the echoes	have some cereal	what skill
five matches to go	I love crunchy celery	he sketched this picture
sit on the benches	off to the cinema	what a legend
fill in the ditches	make a decision	on the stage
unpack your lunches	proceed up the path	a magic spell
hear the wolves cry	are you certain?	plunge into the water
divide into halves	write with a pencil	turn the page
catch those thieves	a recent film	be gentle with him
we did it ourselves	service with a smile	I have an allergy
so many flies	take your medicine	take the register
make three copies	ever since I saw you	a very tall giraffe
armies marching on	recite your poem	he is a giant
no more worries	what a difference	start at the margin
the ferries are delayed	what a sweet kitten	she is a genius
lots of activities	in your kennel	down in the village
no replies	three kippers, please	on the barge
tell no lies	a skinny kid	an original work of art
beautiful babies	let's skim these stones	it's an emergency
20 phrases	20 phrases	20 phrases

One Minute Wonders

	up to 29 Sparking	30–39 Glowing	40–49 Burning	50–59 Sizzling	60+ Red hot!
Score/Date					
Score/Date					

13

gue gui guy

gu

Read the words.

Set 1 (8 words)	Set 2 (16 words)	Set 3 (16 words)	-gue Set 4 (16 words)
guess	**guilt**	guarantee	plague
guest	guild	guitars	vague
guard	guessed	guinea	rogue
disguise	guilds	anguish	vogue
guide	guys	guidelines	brogue
guilty	guile	distinguish	league
Guy	guests	misguided	tongue
guitar	disguised	beguiling	prologue
8 words so far	baguette	guillotine	colleague
	guessing	guardian	intrigue
	guidance	guitarist	vaguely
	penguin	guiltily	monologue
	beguile	disguising	catalogue
	guided	guaranteed	epilogue
	guidebook	extinguished	dialogue
	guiding	disguises	synagogue
	24 words so far	40 words so far	56 words so far

Read the story then draw the picture.

Can you guess who is our mystery guest?

He has a guard and is in disguise.

These clues will guide you to an answer.

Don't feel guilty if you know already …

Yes, it's Guy with a guitar!

Practise writing.

Build your word power.

Well done!
ous
-y
tion
ture
ur
dge
gue gui guy
ge gi gy
ke ki ky
ce ci cy
Plurals

Brilliant! You made it to the next stage!

5

Kenya: First flat tyre (of twenty)! Yes, you guessed it. There is a thorn in the front tyre this time. You stop and repair the puncture with lots of friendly helpers. After all, they feel you are a guest in their country and want to help. The children are truly beguiling and you make friends with them easily. One villager has a guitar and plays for you. You are guaranteed to be surprised in Africa!

15

dge

Fridge on the Bridge

By Charlie

Read the words.

Set 1 (9 words)	Set 2 (20 words)	Set 3 (20 words)	Set 4 (20 words)
fridge	**edge**	pledges	gadgets
bridge	knowledge	gadget	lodgers
judge	badge	stodgy	judges
fudge	hedge	begrudge	knowledge
sludge	cadge	badger	badgered
splodge	ledge	ledger	edgeways
sledge	dredge	midget	prejudge
budge	wedge	fidget	hedgerow
trudged	lodge	dodging	budgie
9 words so far	stodge	judging	lodging
	trudge	dodgy	trudging
	dodge	judgement	misjudged
	ridge	lodger	dredging
	nudge	dislodged	drudgery
	smudge	hedgehog	fidgeting
	wedged	lodgings	fidgeted
	judged	porridge	kedgeree
	ridged	drawbridge	acknowledge
	pledge	dodgeball	sledgehammer
	fledge	nudging	knowledgeable
	29 words so far	49 words so far	69 words so far

	up to 39 Sparking	40–49 Glowing	50–59 Burning	60–69 Sizzling	70+ Red hot!
Score/Date					
Score/Date					

Read the story then draw the picture.

What was a fridge doing on a bridge? It was keeping the judge's picnic fudge from turning to sludge on such a hot day.

"I don't want it to be a messy splodge!" he explained. The judge had pulled his fridge along on a sledge until it hit a pothole and would not budge! Sadly, the judge had trudged home and left the fridge on the bridge.

Practise writing.

Build your word power.

Well done!
ous
-y
tion
ture
ur
dge
gue gui guy
ge gi gy
ke ki ky
ce ci cy
Plurals

Brilliant! You made it to the next stage!

Crossing the Equator: You are on a narrow dirt track that has turned to oozing mud after days of heavy rain. You must trudge along pushing or carrying your bike for a while. Sadly, there's no bridge for you. You had no knowledge it could be quite like this. Great splodges of dirt cover your trousers and your face is smudged where you have wiped your cheek. It seems impossible, but a huge truck makes its way past you through the wet earth and you would love to cadge a lift.

ur

er	ur

Read the words.

Set 1 (13 words)	Set 2 (20 words)	Set 3 (20 words)	Set 4 (20 words)	Set 5 (20 words)
Thursday	**turn**	occur	blurry	survival
nurse	purpose	further	burbled	furthermore
curly	curse	surround	curfew	hurtfully
purple	burst	turkey	outburst	murderess
purse	curve	hurtle	purchase	curlier
turned	burn	gurgle	curving	surrender
surprise	spur	hurtful	burnished	subsurface
church	hurl	surfaced	perturbed	Saturday
burning	lurk	disturb	absurd	surgery
burglar	spurt	lurking	natural	disturbance
hurt	lurch	surprised	surrounded	burnable
murder	fur	murdered	murmuring	overturn
blurted	slur	burgled	urgently	surrendered
13 words so far	curtain	burger	disturbing	burglary
	murmur	hurdle	nocturnal	burgundy
	survive	turtle	absurdly	overburden
	surname	disturbed	purposeful	unsurprising
	return	murky	pre-purchase	survivable
	surface	cursing	murderer	returnable
	burden	furnace	furniture	surprisingly
	33 words so far	53 words so far	73 words so far	93 words so far

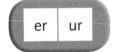

One Minute Wonders

	up to 39 Sparking	40–49 Glowing	50–59 Burning	60–69 Sizzling	70+ Red hot!
Score/Date					
Score/Date					

18

Read the story then draw the picture.

Last Thursday a nurse with long curly hair and a purple purse turned the corner and, to her surprise, saw the church burning. A burglar, who seemed to be hurt, was running away.

"Murder in the church!" she blurted out.

Practise writing.

Build your word power.

Brilliant! You made it to the next stage!

Tanzania: What a night! You have yet more mosquito bites, and you were disturbed by goats bursting into the campsite. They created a huge disturbance and you are still cursing them. The wonderful starry night surprised you, and you were able to turn off your solar-charged torch. Early the next morning, women carrying baskets on their heads wave to you. You are amazed how easily they seem to manage such a heavy burden.

Well done!
ous
-y
tion
ture
ur
dge
gue gui guy
ge gi gy
ke ki ky
ce ci cy
Plurals

Vulture on an Adventure

By Hamish

Read the words.

Set 1 (10 words)	Set 2 (20 words)	Set 3 (20 words)	Set 4 (20 words)
vulture	**mixture**	signature	lecturing
departure	**nature**	venture	capturing
adventure	**furniture**	torture	picturesque
temperature	structure	matured	featureless
moisture	puncture	fractured	curvature
lecture	feature	lectured	textureless
capture	fixture	cultured	miniature
future	mature	maturing	literature
picture	texture	restructure	moisturiser
creature	sculpture	premature	expenditure
10 words so far	fracture	overture	manufactured
	scripture	lecturer	adventurous
	punctured	recapture	agriculture
	pasture	immature	misadventure
	rupture	cultural	manufacture
	culture	featuring	horticulture
	posture	gesturing	architecture
	gesture	capturer	pre-departure
	nurture	uncultured	superstructure
	rapture	venturing	multicultural
	30 words so far	50 words so far	70 words so far

One Minute Wonders

	up to 39 Sparking	40–49 Glowing	50–59 Burning	60–69 Sizzling	70+ Red hot!
Score/Date					
Score/Date					

Read the story then draw the picture.

Vulture was ready for departure. He was setting off on a great adventure. In his part of Africa the temperature was high although there was still moisture in the air. His father had given him a lecture about being careful to avoid capture in the future. He tried to picture what might happen to a creature like him.

Practise writing.

Build your word power.

Well done!
ous
-y
tion
ture
ur
dge
gue gui guy
ge gi gy
ke ki ky
ce ci cy
Plurals

Brilliant! You made it to the next stage!

Zambia: You stop in your tracks to let a herd of wild elephants cross the road. What marvellous creatures! You capture the scene by taking a picture. Another puncture delays your progress, but the temperature is rising and you are glad to stop for a while. You get going but one pannier falls off because the track is so bumpy. Thank goodness you have a high-quality, sturdy bike with 36 spokes, or the wheel might buckle at any time.

Sizzling Syllables! ②

Read the syllables.

Paddle the Amazon review

ool	ply	igh	oax	may	main	quea
bay	cue	wea	fy	flow	mew	stee
floa	strai	gloo	cray	ight	eech	hoa
spy	row	feeb	view	spea	lue	tai

Got it? ☐

New *Cycle Africa* patterns

gue	adge	nur	ture	turb	guin	udge
thur	lur	gui	spur	idge	ture	cur
guit	bur	sur	gues	chur	odge	ture
fur	ture	edge	tur	guil	mur	guer

Got it? ☐

All *Cycle Africa* so far

cent	sur	ture	skim	ance	ges	skel
ture	kit	ence	guit	blur	gis	idge
gui	udge	geon	fur	sket	cel	bur
cip	gel	skit	ture	gyp	guil	skir

Got It? ☐

Fiery Phrases! ②

Guy with a Guitar	Fridge on the Bridge	Murder in the Church	Vulture on an Adventure

Read the phrases.

Set 1	Set 2	Set 3
I need a guide	trim the hedge	look at this turtle
be my guest	on the ridge	enjoy the surf
what a rogue	close the fridge	further on
he is in disguise	look on the ledge	it's urgent
what a good guy	dredge the river	what a surprise
my guinea pig	at the lodge	take a picture
have you guessed	here is my lodger	a lovely sculpture
the guests have arrived	badgers are here	too much moisture
there are no guards	don't fidget	take your temperature
he is my guardian	he has made fudge	a good mixture
I need a guarantee	the judge has arrived	what an adventure
you are being vague	a pretty budgie	in the future
my tongue is burnt	cadge a lift	look at the vulture
the football league	a paint splodge	a great fixture
go to the synagogue	under the bridge	more mature now
the best guitarist	he dodged the tackle	a lot of furniture
a guilty verdict	off to church	a huge structure
the penguin parade	curly brown hair	what a creature
wear this badge	turn around	departure time
I love your sledge	a purple purse	great architecture
20 phrases	20 phrases	20 phrases

	up to 29 Sparking	30–39 Glowing	40–49 Burning	50–59 Sizzling	60+ Red hot!
Score/Date					
Score/Date					

One Minute Wonders

tion

Read the words.

Set 1 (9 words)	Set 2 (20 words)	Set 3 (20 words)	Set 4 (20 words)
fractions	**station**	dictionary	complication
action	**friction**	explanation	circulation
solution	**condition**	competition	decoration
conversation	**protection**	pronunciation	admiration
question	**education**	instruction	adoration
destruction	mention	sensation	hesitation
creation	position	precaution	exhibition
satisfaction	fiction	inspection	preparation
celebration	nation	construction	perfectionist
9 words so far	motion	injection	sensational
	section	fictional	affectionate
	caution	completion	examination
	relation	national	unmentionable
	invention	elevation	organisation
	direction	demolition	evaporation
	affection	population	determination
	election	generation	multiplication
	perfection	information	educational
	devotion	application	communication
	description	invitation	investigation
	29 words so far	49 words so far	69 words so far

	up to 39 Sparking	40–49 Glowing	50–59 Burning	60–69 Sizzling	70+ Red hot!
Score/Date					
Score/Date					

One Minute Wonders

Read the poem then draw the picture.

The fractions are in action to find the right solution
It's like a conversation in answer to a question
There must not be destruction
There can only be creation
As the satisfaction of an answer
Is a cause for celebration!

Practise writing.

Build your word power.

Brilliant! You made it to the next stage!

Botswana: You are too exhausted to wave, smile or have a conversation with the villagers as you pass. A man follows you to tell you that the children are disappointed that you did not stop to meet them. You turn back and spend time with them. They give you fascinating information about their lives, including their education. Such devotion to learning! They obviously have great affection for their teacher. They give you an invitation to stay and share a meal. On the way, you see a herd of ostriches. What perfection!

Well done!
ous
-y
tion
ture
ur
dge
gue gui guy
ge gi gy
ke ki ky
ce ci cy
Plurals

-y

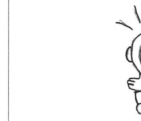

Hungry Baby

By Freddie

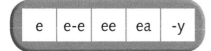

e	e-e	ee	ea	-y

Read the words.

Set 1 (13 words)	Set 2 (20 words)	Set 3 (20 words)	Set 4 (20 words)
pretty	**marry**	century	forty
Holly	**beauty**	February	category
happy	**only**	history	secretary
baby	**ready**	library	**community**
hungry	**story**	army	**accompany**
tummy	**country**	gypsy	**variety**
empty	**any**	hobby	identity
mummy	**body**	jolly	**curiosity**
daddy	**carry**	bully	trophy
very	**many**	rally	messy
busy	**family**	penny	canary
worry	**enemy**	daily	energy
granny	**ordinary**	holly	poetry
13 words so far	**company**	berry	factory
	quality	daisy	contrary
	society	cherry	sympathy
	opportunity	vary	calligraphy
	lady	county	extraordinary
	jelly	pony	inequality
	party	floppy	autobiography
	33 words so far	53 words so far	73 words so far

	up to 39 Sparking	40–49 Glowing	50–59 Burning	60–69 Sizzling	70+ Red hot!
Score/Date					
Score/Date					

Read the story then draw the picture.

Waaah! Pretty little Holly was not a happy baby because she was a hungry baby! Her tummy was empty but her mummy and daddy were very busy. Don't worry! Granny to the rescue!

Practise writing.

Build your word power.

Brilliant! You made it to the next stage!

10

Namibia: A beautiful country! Happily, the route is mostly flat, but you go on too long and your muscles are really achy. Your backside is very sore too, so thank goodness you chose a comfy leather saddle or it might have been worse! You feel very floppy so take a rest under a pretty acacia tree but have to watch out for scratchy thorns, as prickly as any holly bush! It's wonderful seeing such a variety of wildlife.

OUS

For adjectives and adverbs

Famous Fish

By Charlie

Read the words.

Set 1 (9 words)	Set 2 (20 words)	Set 3 (20 words)	Set 4 (20 words)
marvellous	**serious**	**conscious**	rigorous
pompously	various	**disastrous**	non-porous
dangerous	jealous	furious	mountainous
obvious	nervous	odious	luxurious
famous	cautious	generous	carnivorous
humorous	pompous	poisonous	deciduous
envious	monstrous	hazardous	spontaneous
delicious	anxious	glamorous	overanxious
seriously	porous	ferocious	monotonous
9 words so far	bulbous	religious	coniferous
	callous	perilous	furiously
	vicious	courageous	preposterous
	scrumptious	jealousy	adventurous
	luscious	thunderous	humorously
	devious	luminous	tremendously
	curious	vigorous	mischievously
	glorious	mutinous	previously
	outrageous	nauseous	ambidextrous
	hideous	boisterous	omnivorous
	enormous	ravenous	conspicuously
	29 words so far	49 words so far	69 words so far

	up to 39 Sparking	40–49 Glowing	50–59 Burning	60–69 Sizzling	70+ Red hot!
Score/Date					
Score/Date					

One Minute Wonders

Read the story then draw the picture.

"I am marvellous!" said the fish pompously. "I am not dangerous and it is obvious I will be famous very soon. I find it rather humorous that you are all so envious."

"But you are probably delicious too, so watch out, or someone might catch you," his friend pointed out seriously.

Practise writing.

Build your word power.

Well done!
ous
-y
tion
ture
ur
dge
gue gui guy
ge gi gy
ke ki ky
ce ci cy
Plurals

Brilliant! You've done it!

Marvellous! You have completed your hazardous journey. You obtain your final visa at the border and enter South Africa, which is stupendous! Exciting Cape Town, with its famous Table Mountain, lies ahead, along with the glorious South Atlantic Ocean.

Sizzling Syllables! ③

Read the syllables.

New *Cycle Africa* sounds

ture	tion	ous	ture	tion	ous

Got it? ☐

Cycle Africa mix-up

cid	gin	tion	kee	gues	ous
ken	adge	cit	gic	edge	ture
cell	ged	keb	guer	ci	mur
ture	cin	ger	tion	ous	kid
kil	gy	bur	odge	cend	tur
ous	kin	guil	cept	gen	ture
cel	thur	ket	gi	ous	tion
ges	kip	tion	ture	gui	ceed

Got it? ☐

WordBlaze so far

cid	war	atch	gen	gi	own
py	sur	few	broa	ket	way
ous	eath	ture	mai	tion	ives
tue	udge	gle	lee	wor	gis
ight	oose	oes	guil	chur	age
gui	loa	ray	eak	ry	lew
kid	tion	jai	cel	ous	ter
mee	lar	bow	cy	oop	idge
ice	gy	stip	ture	igh	ect

Got it? ☐

Fiery Phrases! (3)

Fractions in Action	Hungry Baby	Famous Fish

Read the phrases. Do you remember all the spelling patterns you have learnt so far?

Set 1	Set 2	Set 3
a fraction of it	the boys are happy	what an adventure
take action now	this bird is pretty	surrender now
off to the station	a jolly clown	raise the drawbridge
ask any question	don't worry	you're urgently needed
the whole nation	some holly	a glamorous film star
don't mention it	what a grumpy lady	picture the scene
what an invention	in that country	don't disturb me
in this direction	so messy	deciduous trees
find a solution	granny has arrived	delicious runny honey
a good description	milky coffee	what a skyscraper
an amazing sensation	use a dictionary	the poisonous snake
timed to perfection	in the factory	please give generously
have a conversation	funnily enough	are you curious
a good education	a bendy toy	dad is anxious
to everyone's satisfaction	don't be nervous	in the future
show some affection	she is furious	such a ridiculous story
it's just a precaution	what a hideous insect	bright red tomatoes
the election is tomorrow	it's so obvious	what a luxurious room
she is a relation	how generous of you	under those bushes
look at the instructions	a ferocious tiger	a glorious day
20 phrases	**20 phrases**	**20 phrases**

One Minute Wonders

	up to 29 Sparking	30–39 Glowing	40–49 Burning	50–59 Sizzling	60+ Red hot!
Score/Date					
Score/Date					

31

Blazing Extras

Read the words.

High frequency words not in patterns			
difficult	separate	gone	sugar
heart	England	even	fashion
length	Europe	taste	beyond
strength	hour	waste	blood
minute	clothes	private	build
favourite	minute	familiar	control
opposite	move	sense	course
pressure	doctor	shoe	court
grammar	else	sign	demand
woman	evening	second	plant
women	water	sure	beautiful

Joe's Oboe

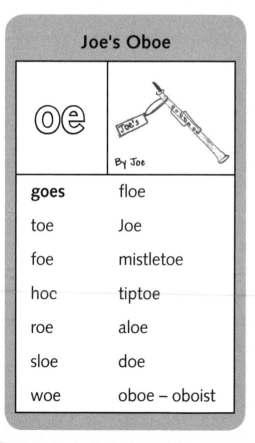

oe

By Joe

goes	floe
toe	Joe
foe	mistletoe
hoc	tiptoe
roe	aloe
sloe	doe
woe	oboe – oboist

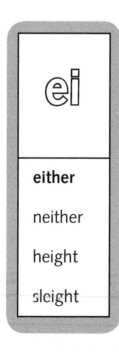

ei

either

neither

height

sleight

Hold your Gold

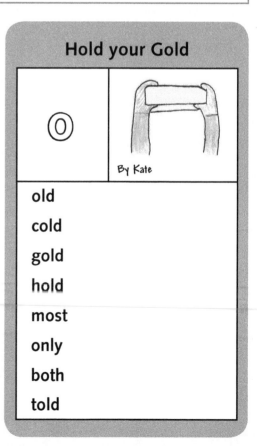

o

By Kate

old

cold

gold

hold

most

only

both

told

Admire the Sapphire

 ire

By Liz

fire	desire	umpire
wire	entire	acquire
tire	aspire	bonfire
hire	empire	ceasefire
mire	haywire	inquire
spire	expire	inspire
admire	rewire	require
dire	retire	backfire
shire	sapphire	quagmire

Exercise is excellent

x	exc

fix	expense	excite
box	exchange	**exciting**
next	exercise	excitement
expect	**example**	excited
explain		excitable
express		excel
extend		excellent
exist	By Anne	exceed
expand		exceeding
expert		except

By Anne

Don't Lie about the Pie

 ie

By Harry

die

lie

tie

pie

Double Trouble

 ou

By George

double

touch

young

trouble

country

cousin

Wild Child

i

By Sam

find	**wild**
kind	mild
mind	unkind
behind	wind
child	climb

White Hot Wonder!

Read the words.

Set 1	Set 2	Set 3	Set 4
potatoes	fudge	dominoes	tragedy
protection	witches	surrender	punctured
kennel	turtle	participate	ditches
purpose	famous	guilty	disguised
capture	sentence	signature	ceiling
benches	mention	replies	population
creature	suggest	evaporation	circulation
barge	sketch	engine	unskilled
dangerous	mixture	fascinate	questionable
sledge	curly	guiding	architecture
success	adventure	absurd	burnable
furious	kisses	kidnapped	kidneys
disturbed	imagine	determination	generously
invention	explanation	agriculture	vague
knives	serious	emergencies	dredging
guest	bulging	manufacture	anticipate
nervous	competition	fidgeting	tremendously
accept	babies	curious	conscious
curved	guitar	murmuring	knowledgeable
trudge	hesitation	ravenous	burglary
20 words	20 words	20 words	20 words

Beat your time!

Set 1	Set 2	Sets 1 and 2

Set 3	Set 4	Sets 3 and 4